The Walking Dead: A Lyric

poems by

Dawn Tefft

Finishing Line Press
Georgetown, Kentucky

The Walking Dead: A Lyric

Copyright © 2016 by Dawn Tefft
ISBN 978-1-944899-16-5 First Edition
All rights reserved under International and Pan-American Copyright Conventions. No part of this book may be reproduced in any manner whatsoever without written permission from the publisher, except in the case of brief quotations embodied in critical articles and reviews.

This book has not been approved, licensed, or sponsored by any entity or person involved in creating or producing *The Walking Dead*, the TV series, graphic novels, or video games.

Editor: Christen Kincaid

Cover Art: Edward J. Moran II

Cover Design: Elizabeth Maines

Printed in the USA on acid-free paper.
Order online: www.finishinglinepress.com
also available on amazon.com

Author inquiries and mail orders:
Finishing Line Press
P. O. Box 1626
Georgetown, Kentucky 40324
U. S. A.

Table of Contents

Section 1: Poems

Endless Summer 1

Disruption 2

Michonne 3

The Women 4

The Archeology of Knowledge 5

The Prison 6

I was Just Another Monster 7

This Prison like a Home 9

Proof 10

Use-value 11

Beth 12

Asshole 13

Glenn Rhee 14

The Farm: A Slow Burn 15

these little gifts 16

Carl Dreams of Going on a Run 17

The Prisoners 19

Prison Diary, 1 20

Prison Diary, 2 21

Prison Diary, 3 22

"That Ain't Us" 23

a zombie forever tries 24

Section 2: Lyric Essay

Daryl Dixon 26

I will not have my life narrowed down. – bell hooks

with special appreciation for Danai Gurira and Norman Reedus

Section 1: Poems

Endless Summer

I've been watching that one zombie stagger
across that field of wheat again and again

a herd of zombies in an endless noisy blur
shaking the trunk of the car where I'm hiding

a zombie cocks its head at me inquisitively
so I aim my knife through the fence link

there's a zombie mother and child pounding
to be let out of the shelter for women

should I go to the well when I know
the water is tainted with bloated zombie

do I open the barn door behind which
my sister prepares her teeth for my throat

even the church pews are filled with zombies
turned while praying, wearing church hats

a zombie is swimming under the water
a zombie is hiding behind the rack of condoms

my father is a zombie and so is my baby
there's no place not streaming with zombies

the forests and the towns and the cities

Disruption

> ". . . . suspend the continuous accumulation of knowledge, interrupt its slow development, and force it to enter a new time, cut it off from its empirical origin and its original motivations . . . towards the search for a new type of rationality and its various effects." – Michel Foucault, *The Archeology of Knowledge*

Zombie studies, teach us that our understanding, of the world, is always open___to disruption. Just ask. *The adopted outlaw as he names: "another man's baby."

Now we write differently, placing punctuation, in unexpected places. Now we dream differently, remembering, what it was once like. *To be "awake."

We write new books, histories. *Of discontinuity:

> *The zombie changes our conversation about church and state. *When it stumbles through court. **And pulpit.*

> *The law of prison is inverted when refugees steal space from the inmates.*

> *When the cop takes advice from the survivalist, and robs like needy people always have, we see a gap. *Between our two logics.*

> *When the zombie shows up on our date, marriage seems like a story. *Told. **To erase community.*

Michonne

a figure in a hooded cape
expertly moves through the woods

kills a zombie with a katana
and stands towering above
yet another woman in need of saving

when we see the samurai clearly
dreads framing a woman's face

suddenly I'm the one being saved
and I think "woman, yes"

she doesn't smile for ages and ages
but when she does, oh, when she does

The Women: Early Seasons

The women must wash clothes, beat them on the rocks, not complain too much, even after catching the fish their damn selves, must not have guns, no, must have guns, must not shoot the guns too much, no, must shoot the guns a lot, must hunt or be hunted, sing in the prison, collaborate with white men when asked, must kiss and fuck, not kiss and fuck, only kiss and fuck the right people, must get permission, not go off on their own, come back quickly when they do, must have babies, not have babies, take care of babies, but not too much, must practice brutal forms of midwifery, thrust and kill and plant and sew and craft.

The Archeology of Knowledge

Beneath the rapidly changing history of governments, wars, and famines, there emerge other, faster-moving histories: the history of escape routes, the history of farming inside a prison, the history of communities kept alive by *vatos*, the history of amputating limbs and scavenging antibiotics, the history of the balance achieved by the human species between hunger and death.

The Prison

We jab through the fence every day
We sift dirt with our fingers
We try to raise our eyes in greeting
We push our voices through tunnels
We hack through the day-to-day
We scrub the top most layers
We talk like people finding each other
We ask mostly physical questions
We fear the trail will go cold again
We steer this grey ship in the forest
We accumulate art from the dead
We jump with routine emergency
We look at the sky like the only oasis

I Was Just Another Monster

"When they're stacked up against the chain-link, you're face-to-face."
"But those sins, I confess them to God, not strangers."

****

"Starting to get afraid that it's easier just to be afraid,"
"spend the rest of our lives staring into a fire and eating snakes."

****

"Turns out it was the tweaker's kid's favorite show."
"The whole world is haunted now."

****

"Loved 'em since I was three years old. Vicious creatures."
"Dragging them around so that I would always know."

****

"Never had a pet pony. Never got nothing from Santa Claus."
"My shit never stopped being together."

****

"I was on the bus and then I got off to help."
"But a bowman's a bowman through and through."

****

"They raped and they killed and they laughed over weeks."
"We let go of all of it, and nobody dies."

****

"And now we've devolved into hunters. I told you, I said it."
"He tells this riddle to people. 'Out of the eater, something to eat.'"

This Prison Like a Home
> *"We took this prison! It's ours!"*

this prison like a home, like a ship in the woods
like a subterranean torture

like a permanent job, like a catacomb
like adventures in Brutalism

this prison that binds us through the nights
giving and draining our pleasure

we work the dirt of a gun and bone farm
and don't know if we can raise children

surrounded by forest and fence, we ask
the sky questions:

> *why do you still appear without limit?*
>
> *when will you bring the music of wings
> and will it be bloodless?*

Proof

when the ravine is too deep
        the wounds are all your own
the sky is circling overhead

plants refuse their soil
        creatures abandon or feast on you
the past is pulling at your leg

there's no life without
        proof compelling you home
your defiance is a rope

Use-value

The houses are all boxes. The houses are boxes that warehouse lace and photos. The houses are boxes that warehouse lace and photos while knives disappear.

While knives disappear, the specter of old Georgia haunts us. The specter of old Georgia haunts us, and we decide to plant beans. We decide to plant beans under the specter of old Georgia and the lace and photos that haunt us.

We drag our feet through the specter. We drag our hands through the dirt and make rows. We make rows in the dirt with the knives that we hoard. We look to the knife-sharp future.

Beth

when the bough breaks

                         a cradle in the prison

song swelling the yard

                a voice when least expected

       criticizing sucky camps

sweetly destroying

           those shacks from the past

a braid lighting the way

                        pouring moonshine on wood

fire after sadness after fire after sadness

Asshole

What do you do with an asshole in the forest? A con artist after you've taken his eye? How do you escape a team of outdoor cats? Or worst of all, your own brother? You might need some of them to get to the other side of the river. You might need their help.

Glenn Rhee

Dumbass,
Clint Eastwood,
you in the tank.

The world is
alleys
and dumpsters.
Counting
the condoms.
Being lowered
into wells.

Stop slowing us
down
like muscly jerks.

We're afraid
of people like us.

The Farm: A Slow Burn

our survivors arrive carrying
a bloody child

one man trades another's life
for medical equipment

the farm is invisibly protected

Herschel's family invites our survivors
to eat at a long, shiny table

"walkers" start showing up
where the farm meets the forest

a forbidden couple has sex
in a deserted pharmacy aisle

a threat starts gathering

is it coming from the outer reaches
or from inside?

the barn door creaks open

these little gifts

a hug or an arrow in the nick of time

      jasper for someone new   to use as a grave marker

            tampons from a ghost town

holding your friend down to cut off a limb

      a man kissing his boyfriend   in front of strangers

           comics foraged from houses

joke about spaghetti Tuesdays   when there's no pasta or calendars

      a life so the rest can make it

Carl Dreams of Going on a Run

I.

I ride a motorcycle out of the prison,
no, a horse

I ride a horse and trample the farm
on my way

while the snakes and the squirrels
and the owls

and the roving bands of wild men
all sing songs

in preparation for my journey

II.

I can hear their voices for miles
and use them as guides

some of the wild men want honor
and jump out from the trees

none know the riddle of the woods

the one who doesn't have much past
to compare with the present
is the one who'll survive to lead

this is how things are now

III.

on my way back, the animals flee
and I wonder what new plague

will I have to have a son, too,
better suited
to this strange new world
causing birds to shriek overhead

The Prisoners

taken by surprise in your own torture
                                      released from the bonds of protection
      how to distinguish locked up from hiding
                        prison from shelter
the pardoners always have guns   and shove you in corners
                                  issuing laws in their boots
ignoring your warnings   "I wouldn't open that if I were you"
                    disgusted by your stench
                            the stink of being hidden by force
     telling you how it is   by stealing your food

Prison Diary, 1

Today a bird flew overhead
and a man came to kill us.

Yesterday, there were no birds
and no men.

Must everything happen at once?

Prison Diary, 2

these new people   whose hands never scrubbed
     mother off of floor   whose heads never touched
          the cool concrete in fear
who haven't smelled   the fridge where prisoners
          stored their own shit
     whose bodies move in   thankful like tourists

Prison Diary, 3

pig squeal in morning—

we get to stay behind fences

is this the new language?

fear/boredom/comfort

"That Ain't Us"

I ain't found that clean line. It's never without repercussions. I've tortured someone in the barn to get information. I've helped strangers with babies, brought loners into the group. I've taken bullets and arrows for children. I've passed people on the road, waving for help, and I never slowed down. I don't want the boy to shoot another boy out in the woods, thinking "this is what boys do now."

A zombie forever tries

A zombie forever tries
to get out of a car.

A grandfather clock
lies dead in the road.

Palms repeatedly beat
against windows.

"We have to stop.
You can be out here too long."

Sunlight shines relentless
through trees.

Half a man crawls
through the grass.

As a gift, someone fixes
the gears of a jewelry box.

The ballerina doesn't turn
until later in the quiet.

Section 2: Lyric Essay

Daryl Dixon

Daryl is drunk and exploding at the farmer's daughter. Moonshine and a talkative young woman who's gone on vacations. These are the catalysts. But the thing that was smoldering underneath is represented by the shack where they've gone to get Beth her first taste of alcohol. Daryl finds himself immersed in the past even in the dead zone of a zombie apocalypse.

Beth is sweet and vulnerable, but also strong in ways that aren't easily measured. She's genuinely interested in who he is, but finds herself falling back on clichés about bad boys, poor people, and hillbillies. Sitting together in a mess like the one he grew up in, even after endangering their lives to get her the very hardest of liquor, she still can't see him.

I find myself perversely cheering him as he both exposes his injuries and taunts her while playing her drinking game. The rules are to say something you've never done. If the other person's done it, they have to drink. If not, you have to drink. His "I've never's:" been outside of Georgia, gone on vacation. And once they've stopped playing the game and he's yelling: relied on anyone for anything.

In these moments, I want good-hearted Beth to really feel shamed by not understanding what it's like to have had to struggle in the ways poor people do. Or in Daryl's case, poor people who've also grown up enduring physical and emotional abuse.

"I never needed a game to get lit before."

What the other characters view as terseness is really much, much more.

It's a lack of knowing how to make himself vulnerable. When you already live a life of extreme vulnerability due to class positioning, every day is another episode in a larger battle. The battle was fixed long ago, and it ain't in your favor. To keep going under these conditions requires toughness. When you try to allow yourself to be vulnerable, you feel the mark of the crosshairs. Instant reminder: the only thing that's gotten you this far is your incredible strength.

It's a lack of material. When you don't have the wide range of formal and informal educational opportunities others have—like going on vacations or traveling outside of the place you were born—you feel you have less to talk about. Or at least less that'll be valued.

It's pride, coupled with fear. Pride in your ability to survive difficult circumstances, which requires intelligence, resilience, and strength. Pride in what other people can't even see about you. Fear that there's something wrong with you, something that destined you to these circumstances to begin with. Or that they've damaged you irreparably.

It's a seething resentment about all of this and needing to talk about it, but knowing that the people you're talking to, these people who aren't even conscious of having acquired a certain ease in navigating the world, won't fully get it. And if they do learn in the ways available to them, they won't want to listen repeatedly. No one wants to be reminded that their positive experiences aren't the results of being more deserving.

Even in the environment of this TV show where everyone loses friends and family to horrors on a regular basis now, people are still shaped by their pasts. Over time, Daryl has become especially empathetic because of his past experiences of trauma. He still struggles because of them, too. Daryl—resourceful and used to hardship—might be the one the other characters believe will be the last man standing, but every day he still has to wake with the by now internalized fear that he was born to be "inferior" and "damaged." That he is and has always been merely surviving.

Dawn Tefft is the author of *Fist* (Dancing Girl Press) and *Field Trip to My Mother and Other Exotic Locations* (Mudlark). Her poems appear or are forthcoming in many journals, including *Fence, Denver Quarterly,* and *Witness*. She holds a PhD in Creative Writing from University of Wisconsin-Milwaukee.

www.ingramcontent.com/pod-product-compliance
Lightning Source LLC
Chambersburg PA
CBHW060225050426
42446CB00013B/3179